COMMON
SENSE

NOT NEEDED

Corrie ten Boom

COMMON SENSE

NOT NEEDED

Bringing the Gospel
to the Mentally Handicapped

CLC ❖ Publications

Fort Washington, PA 19034

Published by CLC Publications

U.S.A.
P.O. Box 1449, Fort Washington, PA 19034

GREAT BRITAIN
51 The Dean, Alresford, Hants. SO24 9BJ

AUSTRALIA
P.O. Box 419M, Manunda, QLD 4879

NEW ZEALAND
10 MacArthur Street, Feilding

ISBN 0-87508-234-3

CONTENTS

"And we urge you, brothers, warn those who are idle, encourage the timid, help the weak, be patient with everyone."

1 Thess. 5:14 (NIV)

INTRODUCTION

Before World War II, I started a work to bring the gospel to mentally disabled people who were not in institutions. They were not able to go to church: they could not understand the sermon. But did they not need the Lord Jesus, just like you and I do? We learn from the Bible that the Lord Jesus has a great love and concern for everyone who is in need, for He said, "Come unto me, all . . ."

Everyone needs the Holy Spirit to understand spiritual truths. I found that when we taught the gospel in an uncomplicated way, the Holy Spirit did not need a high I.Q. to reveal Himself. The mentally disabled whom I taught in the Bible class we had every Sunday afternoon called it their church. We tried to make it as "churchy" as we could to please them!

In this booklet I tell something of what I learned and experienced during the five years I carried on this small work. It was perhaps unimportant in the eyes of the world, but not worthless in God's eyes.

No effort can be valueless when it is in obedience to the command of Jesus: "You must go out to the whole world and proclaim the gospel to every creature" (Mark 16:15, Phillips).

I am sure that earthly values are different from heavenly ones. I believe that the joy among the angels of God is as great when a disabled person is saved as when a V.I.P. gives his heart and life to the Lord. Possibly it is greater; one cannot tell.

A WASTE OF TIME?

Once, in a concentration camp, I was questioned by a Nazi officer. He asked me much about my life, about my work in the Underground and about my spare time. I told him that I had given Bible lessons to mentally retarded people.

"Don't you regard that as a waste of time?" he asked. "Surely it is much better to convert an ordinary person than a disabled one."

This was fully in accord with his Nazi way of thinking. So I told him about Jesus, who had always cared for all who were weak and despised, adding that it might well be possible that the officer and I were much less important in the sight of the Lord Jesus than one of these children. I was sent back to my cell.

The next morning the officer sent for me and said that he had slept badly. He had thought much about what I had said.

"You spoke about Jesus," he said. "I don't know anything about Him. Tell me what you know of

Him." I then spoke of the Lord Jesus as the Light of the World who can lighten our life if we give ourselves to Him and receive Him as our Saviour and Lord. Three days I was questioned and three days I had the opportunity to speak about the gospel of Jesus Christ.

A conversation about the mentally disabled had changed a most dangerous moment for a prisoner into a testimony to the glory of God.

THE OLD, OLD STORY

"How do *you* explain the things of the Bible to the mentally disabled?" I asked teachers at the American schools where they really did their best to teach the gospel.

"Oh, just as we do to typical children," they said, "only simplified, and repeated as often as necessary."

Is an adolescent or an adult with a low I.Q. similar to an average young child? In the slums sometimes we find mentally handicapped persons in their own surroundings. Are their problems the same as the problems of a child?

Yes, many have the same difficulties, but the mentally challenged often have many more. They also have many problems of typical adults. For instance, they are interested in a strike when their father is one of the strikers. Even the severely handicapped daughter of a miner knows about the results of a strike.

They do not comprehend; they do not have the solution: but at the same time they are called upon to share the struggle for life. Who will bring them the answer? Who will tell them that the One who can help them is Jesus, and Jesus alone? He knows the answer to every situation.

I know from experience, for I was in a concentration camp where there was a concentrated mass of problems and misery—but Jesus gave the answer. In this dark place I discovered that demons flee at the name of Jesus; He is Victor. That is the message the *world* must know.

•　　　•　　　•

Kareltje was a little boy twelve years old. He had blue eyes and curly hair. He was one of a large, poor family, and his father was cruel to him because Kareltje was mentally handicapped. He listened as I told the story of the disciples giving food to five thousand people: as the five loaves and two fishes passed from Jesus' hands to theirs, the bread and fish became sufficient to feed the multitude.

Suddenly Kareltje jumped up and, swinging his arms around him, cried, "There is enough! There is plenty, plenty for everyone! Just take, take as much as you like. There is enough! There is plenty!"

Kareltje felt himself one of the disciples. What a joy! "Plenty for everyone."

I wished every child of God rejoiced as Kareltje did about the plenty that we have when taking all from Jesus' hands and passing it on to others.

WHO IS CALLED?

Who should bring the gospel to the mentally handicapped? I asked this question in America of those who understood the need, and always the answer was, "Of course, the ministers."

I do not think so. Ministers know the language of the average population: we cannot expect them to speak the language of the disabled at the same time. There will be people with a special gift for speaking to these childlike ones. There are special difficulties and needs and problems in this particular mission. Sometimes I think I would prefer kindergarten teachers, but they must understand that a mentally challenged adult is different from a child of four. Once I heard a teacher speak to handicapped persons in the same way that she would have done to her kindergarten pupils. These women and men looked in my direction and laughed as if to say, "How silly!"

Children like to hear a story. Disabled people like stories too, but after half an hour's talk about Jesus' love—they will still be listening. They are adults and they must be treated in some way as adults. The language must be plain and clear—no dogmatic talk, no arguments, only the old, old story in plain language. The best way to reach them is by love. Love means understanding, and this love is available (Romans 5:5). God must lead, for without the Holy Spirit no one can bring the message to anybody, handicapped or otherwise. The human spirit fails, except when the Holy Spirit fills.

THE JOY OF
BRINGING THEM THE GOSPEL

The mentally challenged lack common sense, but they also lack analytical criticism which, like a brake, can be a hindrance to the average person. When they trust a teacher (and they do that very soon) they believe everything told them. They just accept what is said.

Once Jake, a tramp, told me that he had seen lightning destroy a tree just in front of him. It was imagination, but I did not argue. I just said, "Jake, if the lightning had killed you, would you have been ready to die, ready to come before God?"

"No," he answered.

I looked at the other boys and asked, "And which of you boys would have been ready to die?" Their heads went down, for the mentally disabled people often express their feelings through their attitude. One boy said, "None of us is ready."

"Well, boys," I said, "we must seek the solution: for we all know that some day the moment will come when we must die." Then I told a story, giving them examples—which is far better than arguing: "Once there was a boy who had to die. He was not at all afraid, for he knew that Jesus loved him and had died for him on the Cross. He loved Jesus for that reason, and he knew that Jesus was preparing for him one of the many mansions in heaven. I am sorry that you do not know what that boy knew."

"But we do," protested one; someone else added, "We are all ready to die, for we all know that Jesus loves us." The whole class was sitting upright at that moment and their faces beamed.

Is it so simple? I doubted it myself for a moment: then the Holy Spirit said to me, "The jailer of St. Paul received the same answer: 'Believe on the Lord Jesus Christ, and you will be saved.'"

How simple is the gospel!

CONFESSION OF GUILT

I had had no experience when I started "church" for mentally handicapped adults. Now, for some weeks we had held our weekly service. So there they were, sitting before me. That Sunday Joan was sitting near Jake. In the midst of my message I saw that Joan could not resist putting her arms around the dirty neck of Jake. She held her face close to the unshaven cheek of the tramp. What should I do? My assistant saw the embarrassing situation. With a serious face, she came to me and said. "I want to tell you something. This morning I was in a church, and I saw all the gentlemen sitting in their pews on one side and the ladies on the other side. We have a real church here, so why do ladies and gentlemen all sit together?"

I answered quite seriously. "I had forgotten, but indeed we are having a real church service. Come, gentlemen and boys, you sit on the right side, the girls and ladies on the other side."

Everyone obeyed, and the love-sick couple was separated; but the problem was only solved for the moment. That week Jake and Joan went into the woods for mischief. Fortunately, the director of social work found them there and told Jake that if he did this again he would be sent to prison. Joan was sent to the institute, where she was given daily work under good leadership.

The next Sunday when I was preaching, Joan ran to me. Her whole face was excited. She had been into mischief, had been scolded for it, and was very upset. She broke into my sermon, laid her arms around me and sobbed: "I have been so naughty. I went for a walk with Jake and I will never, never do it again."

A person often has a big ego. My first thought was one of irritation at losing the thread of my message through the interruption. But then I understood that this demonstration was a very plain form of public confession of guilt. My assistant helped me again. She took the hands of Joan, which I could not get loose, and said, "I'm glad, Joan, that you told this to Miss ten Boom. Let's go into the corridor and ask the Lord Jesus to forgive. Then we can go and have a drink of water."

They left, and after a few moments I rediscovered the thread of my sermon.

WHO IS NORMAL?

It was winter. Holland was occupied by the Germans. We were sitting around the stove before the service began. A girl entered and said, "I hate all Germans, and my father does too."

"That is not right," said Herman.

"Why not?" she replied, "They are our enemies! They have taken away our food! They have taken my brother to Germany! They have . . ." and a list of crimes followed.

"Hate is not right," repeated Herman. "Jesus says, 'You must love your enemies.'"

"I can't," said the girl.

"Jesus does, and He can teach you," said the boy.

That same evening I was at a dinner party with many "normal" Christians, and the conversation was about the Germans. "We are not only allowed to hate," said the leader of the dinner party, "we must hate."

Who is normal, and who handicapped?

HYPNOSIS?

"Your work among the mentally disabled is nothing more than hypnosis," people told me. "They have no common sense, and no criticism. They just believe whatever you tell them."

"I believe in the Holy Spirit," I answered.

·   ·   ·

During the war, bombs were falling on Haarlem. One fell on a house near where Jo was living. Jo was a mentally challenged woman of thirty-two, a nervous and fearful creature. The next Sunday she came to church and told me what had happened.

"The bomb fell and all the windows broke and there was a terrible noise, and . . ."

"What did you do?" I asked.

"I was so frightened, but I just thought of one thing."

I understood what she meant by one thing—she meant prayer. "What happened then?"

"Jesus took all my fear away!"

·   ·   ·

At those moments when bombs were falling, how many "normal" people thought of praying? There was no one there to put this idea into Jo's mind by suggestion, or hypnosis. No human being, true—but Jesus was there.

THE LORD'S SUPPER

Once the father of a mentally disabled girl spoke to me: "Why can my daughter never partake of Communion? Is the Lord's Supper only meant for certain of God's children?"

"Pray about it!" I answered, "I'll do the same." That week I discussed the matter with a minister. God showed us that it was His will for them to receive the Lord's Supper as well as Baptism. About fifteen disabled people I knew, who loved the Lord, were baptized and received the Lord's Supper. Never have I received such a blessing from the Sacraments. There was earnestness and joy.

A boy continued to kneel and would not rise. I took his hand and brought him back to his chair, but he kept his eyes closed. In this way, he wanted to preserve the blessing and joy of that moment!

. . .

We in Holland have a long, imposing liturgy for the Holy Communion. Before we all went to the Lord's Supper, I translated the dignified words into their language. 1 Corinthians 11:29 states: "He that eateth and drinketh unworthily, eateth and drinketh judgment to himself, not discerning the Lord's body."

I explained the text with the following story: "Once there was a lady who went to the Lord's Supper. But she did not believe that Jesus had suffered on the Cross for her, and she did not love Him at all. What do you think about that?"

"That is terrible," they responded.

"Yes, I think so too," I said, "and the most serious thing is that God also thinks it is terrible. He says: 'It is far better *not to go at all* than to take the bread and wine without loving Christ. For if one does so, I must punish him.' If you don't believe, don't go."

They understood.

CONFESSION OF SIN

We were together in our church room and I spoke about the meaning of *sin*. "Do you all know what the word 'sin' means?"

They told me they surely knew. It was disobedience, bad words and ugly thoughts. It was lying, killing, beating, swearing, unbelief in Jesus Christ. "Have you ever sinned?" I asked.

"Never," was the unexpected answer from Marie, a mentally handicapped woman. Her whole face was radiant with pride. I tried to argue, but could not convince her. Then I spoke of the love of Christ and she told me: "I know that Jesus loves me so that He died on the Cross for me. I love Jesus and tell Him everything." Her whole face was beaming with joy.

I knew that Marie had only some months to live—she had cancer. I was not afraid that she was not ready to appear before God's throne. Why Jesus died on the Cross she did not understand, but she was thankful for His love—perhaps more thankful and glad than many good, mentally able Christians who have a sound theology but whose eyes do not sparkle as Marie's do when speaking of Jesus' love.

PROPHETS AND PRIESTS

Some mentally handicapped people can understand at times more than one would expect. For the sake of experiment, I taught them the star constellations. After some practice, they were able to lay white beans on the table to represent Orion and the Big Dipper. Later, I took them for a walk in the evening and showed them the real Orion. In excitement, they shouted, "Look, it is just like our white beans!"

I found that they had not understood at all what I had meant by the white beans.

To teach them spiritual truths was far more successful, for here we experienced the Holy Spirit working with their spirits. Common sense was not needed.

I had told them about the difference between priests and prophets. I asked Marie if she had understood it. She replied, "Oh, yes; that is very easy. Both are messengers between God and men. A priest stands with his face to God. A prophet has his back to God and his face toward men."

It was rather a good answer, but I was not sure that she had really understood, so I asked: "What was I today when I gave you the Bible lesson?"

"A prophet," she answered, "for you brought God's message to us. But you were also a priest when you prayed together with us and asked the Lord to make our hearts ready for His love."

PRAYER

What is prayer? The typical person may understand and know, but how may we make the mentally handicapped understand? A class sat before me: their ages ranged from sixteen to forty-seven. Childlike? Yes. The woman in the first seat had the understanding of an eight-year-old, although she was born thirty-five years ago.

That evening when I stopped explaining, I knew that I had failed. Nobody had understood what praying meant. The next week the girls came to the class quite excited. They had heard over the radio that Holland's little Princess had been baptized. They had a lot of questions to ask.

"Why did the Princess cry?" "Does baptizing hurt?" Some described the Princess lying on a beautiful pillow which the Queen had embroidered; their imaginations were great.

I tried always to combine my lessons with the subject that occupied them, so I let them tell all they knew and then I asked: "What do you think about Prince Bernhard? When the little Princess learns to talk and tries to tell her papa about her experiences as a little child, will the Prince take time to listen?"

"Yes, of course," they answered.

"Surely not. Would such a great Prince listen to a conversation about broken dolls and gathering flowers?"

"Oh, yes! He will," they shouted.

"Why?" I asked.

"Because he loves his baby Princess!"

"Yes, I believe that too," I said. "And you know, that is why Jesus will listen when people tell Him everything. It is because He loves you and me."

"Me too?" asked one woman, with a new light in her eyes.

"He loves you too! And what if the little Princess would never talk to her father? The Prince would be very unhappy. In the same way, Jesus is unhappy when you do not talk to Him. He is happy when you tell Him about your needs, your joy, your hunger, your pain, your fears. He will listen, just as the Prince will listen to Princess Beatrix when she wants to tell about a new pair of shoes, a sore little finger, a piece of chocolate, or being scared of a big dog. Telling Jesus everything—that's prayer."

CHURCH DISCIPLINE

Before a dignified assembly of theologians and other important people, I told about bringing the gospel to the mentally disabled and the possibility of giving them the blessing of the Sacraments.

"But what about church discipline?" they asked.

· · ·

We had the Lord's Supper in the magnificent cathedral of Haarlem. About a hundred Christians joined our special church in order to let our people know that there was a congregation accepting them. When communicants went to the table, Jantje left the pew and wanted to join them. I stopped him and said. "No, Jantje, you are not permitted to go; you know that." Then Jantje took his hat and left the church. His eyes were dark with anger.

Next week I asked, "Jantje, do you know why Willem was allowed to go to the Lord's Supper? He had told me that he loves Jesus! Do you love Jesus too, Jantje?"

"No, I don't," was his answer.

"Do you know," I asked, "why Annie was allowed to partake? She prays every day and tells Jesus all she needs and all she enjoys. Do you pray, Jantje?"

"No, I never do."

"You see, Jantje, that is why you were not allowed to go to the Lord's Supper. But from now on, if you pray and love Jesus, then the next time you may join us. Won't you ask Jesus to come into your heart?"

Jantje did. From that moment on, he began to pray; and when we talked about Jesus' love, his eyes sparkled with joy.

Yes, we had church discipline, but of a special order.

ANOTHER WORLD WAR?

Although their minds have not developed, often the mentally disabled can be just as physically strong as others. Jan and Henk were fighting before the church service. It took rather a strong effort to separate the wrestling men. I got Jan outside the building; Henk was allowed to join the church service. But I was not surprised when, after church, I found Jan outside the door and he told me his plans: he had made up his mind to break a chair on the guilty head of Henk.

I prayed for wisdom and the Lord gave it. "Listen, boys," I said, "do you know that this is the way the war started? Two men quarreled, some took the side of one, and some the side of the other. This grew and grew until two countries were fighting a war. Then other countries joined in, and now we have a World War."

Jan and Henk looked very worried. They knew perfectly well what a World War meant—we were in the very midst of one. The faces of all their peers, who had gathered around, looked anxious. What were they to do? One World War was bad enough, and now Jan and Henk perhaps had started another.

"I wish I knew someone who could help us," I said with a deep sigh.

Henk suddenly got an idea. "I know someone," he shouted. "The Lord Jesus!"

"Sure, He can help us. Let us ask Him!"

We closed our eyes, and I asked the Lord Jesus to forgive Henk and Jan and to give them love instead of hatred in their hearts. All went home satisfied.

That same evening, while I was pulling the curtains to prepare for the blackout, I saw Henk and Jan walking before the house arm-in-arm. Both smiled at me and seemed to say, "All is well now. There won't be another World War!"

PUSHING AWAY

I had spoken to our boys about prayer. Jake, the
tramp, accompanied me home. First he had told
me how he had begun a business. He had taken the
door of his room and chopped it up into small pieces
to make firewood. Then he sold the wood, going
from door to door. This was good business in Holland during the war. Cost: not one cent. Profit:
enough money for many weeks. It was not easy to
persuade Jake that what he did was stealing.

"Jake, do you know what prayer is?" I asked.

At first he was silent. "Do you mean like this?"
Jake asked hesitatingly. "Often I feel something I
can't push away."

"That's it, Jake! Praying is asking Jesus to push
away what you cannot push yourself. Jesus can do
everything, and He loves you so much that He wants
to push away the bad things in your life."

The next day I had something I could not "push
away." I was downhearted and the spirit of worry
was in my heart. Then I remembered the conversation with Jake and I asked, "Lord Jesus, will You

push away the worry?"
    And He did.

BEHOLD, YOU ARE THERE

Apart from running a church for the mentally disabled, I had clubs and classes for them. One of the most faithful members was a man named Roel.

Roel had low self-esteem and tried to compensate for it by boasting of all his abilities. He was a broad-shouldered man of twenty-eight years.

"My, the police were happy that I was so active," he once told me. "A very bad man went into a bush with a little girl. I told a policeman, 'Go into that bush; there is a job for you to do.' Later he said, 'Thank you, Roel, for having warned me just in time.'"

I knew Roel long enough to understand what that story meant. Roel himself had committed the crime and was found by the police. The mentally handicapped often tell of a sin that burdens their heart but will attribute it to someone else. They are always the imaginary hero who has discovered the crime!

"Roel," I said, "don't you know that God is angry when you do such things?" I spoke about God's judgment of sins that evening. When next I had a talk with Roel, a minister who visited the class was present. Roel appeared visibly afraid.

"Is God here?" he asked.

"Sure He is."

"Then I will go home as quickly as I can."

"But He is everywhere. At your home too."

The minister tried to explain God's omnipresence. "Roel," he said, "the sun shines here, the sun shines at home too. It is the same sun. There is air here and air at home. It is the same air. God too is everywhere at the same time!"

Roel had always shown little respect for logical talking—a safe attitude to cover his lack of common sense. He smiled and said, "The sun is not God. The air is not God. I am going home, for God is here."

"Roel, listen," I said. "Whether you like it or not, God is in your home and He sees everything—even what you did in the bushes. Roel, God is angry with you, and there is no escape. The only thing to do is to tell Him that you are sorry and ask His forgiveness in Jesus' name. Then ask Jesus to come into your heart again. He will make you strong and good."

And Roel did.

THOSE WITH
DOWN'S SYNDROME

I like those with Down's syndrome. Often they are such lovable people. Why does God allow them to be born to quite healthy parents, who neither drank nor committed those sins which so often cause the birth of handicapped children? I don't know. Those with Down's syndrome are sometimes as sweet as very little children, while their I.Q. may be exceedingly low.

Anton had Down's syndrome. He could neither speak nor walk along. He was, for a very short time, in my class. He listened to my Bible stories, but when I spoke too long to suit him, he yawned like a monkey. I did not know how much Anton really understood.

Once I took his hand and touched his five fingers one after another; then I said, "Jesus loves Anton so much." The next week, Anton immediately saw me. He took my hand and, with his fingers outspread, he looked at me with a face full of longing. "Jesus loves Anton so much," I repeated, touching a finger at every word. Then I taught him to do it himself. Every week after that, Anton showed me with his fingers how much Jesus loved him. The last time I saw him, I told him, as he touched his left fingers with his right hand, "Jesus loves Anton so much. How thankful I am for that! You too, Anton?"

"Yes," said Anton, as his face lit up.

It was the only word I ever heard from Anton. It is the most worthwhile word that *any* person can speak to the Lord Jesus.

THE OCEAN OF LOVE

I shall never forget what a minister told me about a developmentally disabled boy, Toontje, who attended his church services regularly and was always seated in the first pew.

"I wonder if Toontje understands one word of what I say," he sometimes said to his wife.

Once he preached about the abundant love of God that passes all understanding. Suddenly, he saw a look of great joy upon Toontje's face. The minister almost forgot the rest of the congregation; he spoke as if to the boy alone about the ocean of God's love in Jesus Christ.

The next morning he said to his wife, "I cannot forget Toontje's happy face; I am sure that he has grasped something of the joy of God's love. I am going to visit him this morning."

When he arrived at the home, the door was opened by Toontje's mother. "This morning," she told him, "we found that Toontje had died in his sleep." The minister saw on the face of the dead boy a look of heavenly joy and peace. Toontje's heart had broken with joy as he grasped so much of the love of God.

Do we not all need the Holy Spirit to enlarge our hearts to contain only a little more of the joy unspeakable and full of glory—God's abundant love in us? Otherwise our hearts would burst with happiness!

JOY IN HEAVEN

Bringing the gospel to developmentally disabled people is not popular work in the eyes of the world. To convert a "big shot" is more important than to change a disabled person who cannot organize a mission, start a drive to collect money, write books, or do what certain others could do.

Does heaven have the same standards as on earth? Thankfully not.

I know that before going to heaven, Jesus' last words were, "Go ye—and preach the gospel to every creature." And I think that the mentally handicapped have received a special grace to enable them to understand the gospel.

I believe that when a mentally disabled person is converted, the joy before the angels of God is as great as when a "big shot" gives his heart and life to Jesus. It is possible that the joy is greater—heaven differs greatly from earth. One can never tell.

"FINALLY, BRETHREN—!"

My experiences in four years' work in Haarlem brought me into contact with only a handful of the many developmentally disabled of the world. I reached only a few of the handicapped in one town in one small country. Besides this group of people, there are all the emotionally disturbed, the shell-shocked, and those suffering from mental illness. What difficult problems are these that I have not touched upon!

The woman with the seven demons was a difficult problem. Did Jesus not succeed?

Bringing the gospel is not *our* work—it is *God's* work. He will use us who are ready to obey.

God's Kingdom will come. It is great to fight in a war knowing beforehand that your King is the Victor.

This book was produced by CLC Publications. We hope it has been helpful to you in living the Christian life. CLC is a literature mission with ministry in over 50 countries worldwide. If you would like to know more about us, or are interested in opportunities to serve with a faith mission, we invite you to write to:

CLC Publications
P.O. Box 1449
Fort Washington, PA 19034